STRING THEORY

STRING THEORY
BY

DOMINIC J P NELSON-ASHLEY

For further information
on Dominic JP Nelson-Ashley,
please visit
www.djpnelsonashley.com
www.blackwords.org

First published 2019 by Ek Zuban
c/o 52 Carlow Street
Middlesbrough
TS1 4SD
United Kingdom
www.ekzuban.org.co.uk

EK ZUBAN
ISBN 978-0-9935006-2-6

Edited by Bob Beagrie
Cover image by Jamie Wisdom
Cover design by Jamie Wisdom

Thank You.

INTRO

This book is dedicated to

my father
who wanted me to be
a preacher in church on Sundays,
to whom I said – no, that isn't me.

And my friends
who said,
'That thing you do,
shouting down the phone at people
about what you believe.
That's quite a lot like what a preacher does.'

CONTENTS:

4.WORK + MONEY

5.RACE

6.SEX+RELATIONSHIPS

ALLERGIES
ROLL

7.DEATH
#DEATH
NO QUEUE JUMPING
GUITAR HERO
PEOPLE
ENOUGH
PUNCTUAL

8.END
ROCKET-MAN
A BIGGER BANG
JOKE OUTRO
A BIGGER QUESTION

MEN DON'T TALK

My first book was semi-autobiographical.
This one, with its multiple voices,
is a work of complete fiction.

However,
the story I am about to tell is true and is the reason
why I wrote this book.

My head pounded.
Hard.
I heard his name screaming in my head.
This noise was deafening, debilitating.
I phoned his house.
His mum said he was out.
She'd get him to call me as soon as she saw him again.

We never saw him alive again.

It is not my place to go over the why's,
the how's and all the details.
There is no point.
There is no point on trying to analyze why.

or maybe there is.

Boys and Men don't talk enough, that is well known.
One in four people will have a mental health problem
at some stage in their lives.

Maybe reading this book will help someone.

JOKE

This,
like many things in a messy life,
started with a joke
and got out of control.

KNOWNS REFIX

This is not a poetry book.

This is a science book disguised as a poetry book.

It must be.

It's got numbers, conundrums and bits that need a calculator

to add together what we know, what we know we don't know

to find out, after much soul-searching, we know nothing.

1.BEGINNINGS

THE BIG BANG

How did this universe start?

A Big Bang?
A lightning strike?

An element of danger:
A rocking cable car over a ravine or choppy sea?

The holding of hands?
A place on stage?

A dream of a spotlight,
one mic-stand and an SM58 microphone?

FAIRYTALES

The truth is -

Fairytales are fantastical stories,
life without the rough edges.

Fairytales are life with sharp corners,
shattered mirrors.

Stories are data with soul,
lies that tell the truth.

Shame is the fear of disconnect.

Can we measure
courage? connection? compassion?

Can we count up
vulnerability?

Can we sing:
I am worthy of love,
with the courage to be imperfect?

The truth is -

I have one million 46 thousand 333
words and counting.

The truth is -

I live in a gingerbread house
with a mirror that lies to me.

The truth is -

I will make up any kind of gibberish
to get out of talking about my feelings.

2. BIRTH

EYES

Remember,
she's got your eyes.

Whatever happens next -

Remember,
she's got your eyes.

ART

I

Labels are like art.
Put them in a sterile frame, hang it up,
stick it in a corner gathering dust
or cut them up, make a collage of something new.

II

People don't like the way I wobble,
the way I talk slow, my twisted knackered body.
They don't understand my reason for being here.
I don't know either.
If it was up to me I would've aborted myself.

I get in everyone's way. I take up too much space.
I take up too much time.

Complex needs, expensive support.
I see the upside down words on the report pages.

Red, green, black ink.

I've seen it so many times, I've painted it in my memory,
stuck it on my frontal lobe.

But that's what I deserve:
The scraps, the residue
cos I shouldn't be here.

Complex needs, need I say more.

III

It turns out, making babies is a complex thing.

Sperm are racers.
5 mm per minute,

five body lengths of the sperm per second.

If scaled up to the size of a salmon,

that would be them swimming along

at 500 miles an hour,

or a whale doing 15,000 miles an hour.

One winner to fertilise the egg
has to beat 40million others.

No wonder I look a bit knackered.

But that means

I'm a winner
and a fighter
and unique.

I am
more than
facts, figures
and upside down writing.
I am here.

IV

I make art.
I hang it up in galleries where everyone can see.
I don't care if people like them or not.

BUMPS

We did all the right things, didn't we?
We exercised, synchronised our bodies and minds,
put aside the arguments, didn't we?

Danced at the news before the belly got big.
Felt the rosy glow before visible.

Ready to be adorned in long spacious flowing dresses.

Cooking for 2.
Together eating for 3.

Feel it grow feel it spread.

We are like everybody else -
normative statistics.
We are all we ever wanted -
a mathematical non-conundrum
1 plus 1 equals 3.

Fragile hands.
Dainty boots.
Half the room pink, half the room blue.
'Sex unknown, doctor's orders'

Hear the heart?

*

Knitted boots.
Thimble mittens remain in the draw.

Ping -
eBay bid accepted.
'Brand new never used
Still in the bag they came in.'

We are outliers on the curve.
We ask why:

Drunk girls who do everything wrong,
push out unwanted babies without blinking?

We ask why:

When we did everything right,
followed the rules -
we have no child?

We did everything right –

Now she's
cooking for 2
eating for 1

with a large slice of cake for dessert.

ROOM

I was in the room when my daughter was born.
I thought if there was ever a time
the Mrs was gonna slag me off, curse me out,
this would be it.

Between the pushing, deep breathing, screaming,

but she never did.

She crushed my hand though.
Remind me never to arm-wrestle her.

BEES

We preach the gospel of financial prudence
and get handsomely rewarded for it.

You've got contracts - great mathematical conundrums.
You've got paper that means you'll get paid.

I believe.
The Government believes.
You think it's smoke and mirrors.

You are handsomely rewarded with
a young ambitious girlfriend.
You are handsomely rewarded with
a young ambitious wife.

She has wide childbearing hips.
You have a baby.
You dote on her.

Business is good.
Many contracts.
Many pieces of paper.
Expand.

Your baby dies.

You believe.
The Government believes.
I think it's smoke and mirrors.

You re-mortgage the house.
You have another baby.
The baby lives.
You spend time with the baby.

There is the paperwork.
There is the re-re mortgage.
There is a young ambitious wife.

I believe.
You believe.
The Government thinks it's smoke and mirrors.

There is -
the paperwork,
the baby who became a girl,
the re-re-re mortgage.

*

There is the young ambitious wife.
There is the divorce.
There is your pot belly, weight gain –
the circumference of which is?

There are the coded messages
from phones hidden in bushes,
left in an array of patterns,

avoiding creditors –
people looking at paperwork of
re-re-re-re mortgages.

Your baby
is now a woman.
She lives
in a different home.

Your ex-wife
is ex-directory.

You keep bees -
simple creatures, 1000s in one hive,

they fly in complex mathematical patterns,
no paperwork.

3.LIFE

TWO SIX NINE

You know I'm on your team, right?
All day everyday.
24 hours a day 7 days a week.
24-7
25-8
26-9
Anyway it adds up, right?
Men like us take the heaviest hits, the hardest blows.
Supposed to stand resolute, are we?
Tall and proud, are we?
Whilst the internal masonry of the head crumbles.

That ain't right.

I'm on your team.
You got that?
Team
24-7
25-8
26-9
I don't care who knows it.
I already shouted it at anyone who will listen.

So we can sit and say nothing
or talk about trivial things:

The last game.
The next game.
The best route.
The price of petrol.
The price of a shit pint.

Until we get to the truth -
Why you're feeling the way you're feeling
however long it takes.

Know this and know this strong -
I'm on your team
24-7
25-8
26-9.

STRENGTH

Remember
how you
shared too much
with the kids,
when
all they wanted -
was silent strength?

WHICH WAY ROUND, BROTHER?

My brother.
Same mother same father.

He's good at the jokes.
Always has been, always will be, from Day-One,
from the day they brought him home.

God's jester.
I'll drink to that.

Brother,
which way round are your legs supposed to be?
Did the stork have a crash on the way over?

Spinning around,
cheaper than a spinning top,
yoyo or marbles
and much more fun.
I'll drink to that.

One arm, the other's fucked,
never be able to look after himself.

That's my brother.
Same mother same father.

God's jester.
I'll drink to that.

Twists and turns
on the rugby pitch.

Is he injured? No.
My Crip' always walks like that.

Twisted spastic boy's an alcoholic:
It's the pain, it's in his head or his legs.
Which way round is that?
Spinning like the old days, brother?
Always up for a laugh?
I'll drink to that.

Can't get a girl.
Can't keep it up.
Can't hold down a job.

Brother.
Same mother same father.
I'll drink to that.

Get a few pints down his neck and he'd pull.
He's just shy.
I'll even get the first round in.

Dabbled in a little of the heavier stuff, did he?
Silly boy.
Self medicated?
Silly boy.

Same mother same father.
God's jester.
But he prays to some earth deity
cos he's not in a wheelchair?
It don't make no sense,
but I'll drink to that.

Doctors overprescribed -
Brother's gone teetotal,
gone cold turkey,
gone vegan,
won't touch a drop.
Won't touch anything.
More for me.
I'll drink to that.

Runs around after Pa.
Good at running around after people.
I'll drink to that.

Father died.
He was by the bed side.
He says he's got it sorted.
Canny bloke my brother.
I'll drink to that.

Runs around after Ma.
Good at running around after people.
I'll drink to that.

He said 'mum's turned blue, where was I?'
'In the pub, you got my number,' I said.
It's my office. My home from home,
when I'm not living at mum's home.

*

Brother's off to his own flat.
When did that happen?

It's up 10 flights of stairs,
how does my cripple get up there?

Brother's got a wife?
When did that happen?

Brother's got a job
and his own accountant?
When did that happen?

I'm pleased for him.
Looks like he's sorted.
I'll drink to that.

He's got a temper though,
When did that happen?

Yells at me, calls me things.

I should twat him, I'm the bigger brother.
Same dead mother same dead father.
We could make up over a pint,
I'd even get the first round in.
I'd drink to that.

Say's he doesn't do pubs!
He says my brain's hollow.
More room for the booze then.
He's good at the jokes.
Always has been, always will be, from Day-One.
God's jester.

I don't know why he laughs at me though.
Anyway,
I'll drink to that.

FASHION FORWARD

Why aren't you fashion forward?
Your hair is too long
but if you want to keep it,
you could trim it, cut it,
keep the length, tie it back.
You could look
in a certain light
with a following wind
and the sepia gauze haze of six o'clock in the morning,
and squinting -
pass off as a Parisian photographer.

The 'two-shirt no-trouser look' at 4am
was never in vogue.

The string vest,
white pants, grey socks,
batman slippers on a park bench at 3am
was never in vogue.

It was never stated by the style-makers as fashionable.

If only you put the effort in.
You got some issues, have you?
What's that got to do with how you look to the naked eye?

Talking of naked -
shuffling around in a ripped dressing gown
with nothing else underneath
with ice cream dribbling down your chin at 2am

is not a winning catwalk combination.

If you want to strut along the dingy streets of Grangetown,
do it with panache,
between the hours of 9pm to midnight on the weekends
at a stag party
or one of those haute couture evenings in Milan
and get paid for it.

Be truly fashion forward.

That look
That look
That look
That you call 'individual'
Call 'doing your own thing'

Nobody wants to see that:

The police
Your dealer
Your local off-licence
Social services
Nobody wants to see that

With a little more effort
You could be so
Fashion forward.

GOOD

Nobody
knows how
good
I was today.

BED OF NAILS

Thank you for your generosity.
How can I ever repay you?

I've had trouble sleeping for years,
a chiropractor would be good -
someone to crunch my bones back into place
after all those nights huddled up in street doorways,
alleyways by the bins.

But you've gone one better.
How can I ever repay you?

I dreamed of exotic beauty spa treatments in the rain.
My damp clothes were hot massage towels
worn in the after-glow.

I dreamed of watching
magical Indian healers working on me.
Old Hindu fakirs aligning my body and mind
in perfect harmony.

But you went one better.
How can I ever repay you?

The flat park benches weren't doing me any good,
not helping my curved spine.
You took them away, shut the park at night
gave the warden a bonus for doing so,
it's probably for the best.

Teach me.

You are so wise,
so thoughtful
how can I ever repay you,
when all you want for me to do
is learn the tricks of magical Indian rope men?

Spikes that come out of the ground at night
at my favourite street sleeping spot -
Therapeutic bed of nails,
such thoughtful luxury.
I feel blessed.

How can I ever repay you?
When all I've learnt to do is disappear.

STEPPING LIGHTLY

You throw words around without thought,
scatter them with no planning.
You have never seen or heard true pandemonium?
Have you ever seen a head break a staircase?

You say I'm a violent man,
but you've only heard my rumbling deep bass voice:

On football terraces.
Getting money back on a bad deal.
Getting rid of insurance cold callers.
Improving service at restaurants.

You like it then, don't you?
You've never seen blood pouring out
where blood shouldn't be seen.

I grew up in a house like that.

Chants of -
Pick a window, you're leaving.
Pack your bags, you're leaving,
take the glass splinters with you.
Pack a nightgown, your deflated football,
you're leaving through a bolted door.

I put my fingers in the ears when you talk.
Prima donna tones, my brain explodes.

I can't live on tiptoes over eggshells,
over skulls

or you thinking I'd do that.
I've worked too hard
not to be
what you think
I could be

with this voice
with this body
with this strength.

Be a diva, soprano, tenor on your own.
Watch me as I walk out stage exit left
pianissimo baritone cadenza –
no crescendos, no bodies broken.

Why?

It comes down to trust.
There's a way of singing,
there's a way of living,
there is a way of living without living.

I've been there.

Catch the bouncing ball of your own speech.

You throw around heavy words too lightly.

ANGELS

I am
running out of angels,
running out of lawyers,
running out of listeners,
running out of meat and 2 veg,
pot noodles, spliffs and friends,
running out of tv box sets
running out of places to sleep

and

I am tired,
tired through to my bones,
tired of not knowing what an angel looks like.
Been on my knees too many times.
Praying,
scrambling through the dirt for the last blunt
to smoke some temporary hope.
That's when I see my angels.
That's when I know their faces are running to me.

HOUSE

Remember when your mum said,
you were 'the man of the house now'
but you still had to ask her
for pocket money?

LABELS

OCD?
Don't care
Labels are like jackets, t-shirts.
You can change them when you like.

You work with kids, yeah? Kids like me, yeah?

Don't know whether to call you mate, dad or elder brother?
Can I tell you stuff?

You got me working hard.
Chat long, chat large.

I'm moving on.
I'll be in touch.

Love chatting, me.

Thanks for the loan of the suit.
Honestly?
It's a bit baggy.

Everything's alright.
I got off the charges.

Mum's still worried though.
Real dad's not much cop for a cop.

*

I still don't know whether to call you mate, dad or bro?
Do you fancy my mum?

I got a job.
They like the way I chat - easy going.

It's all legit.

I can sell anything, me.
Windows, cars, what's in the window, what's in the car.

I got caught.
Might get banged up.
Shitting bricks.

Can I borrow your suit again?
Did you get it dry-cleaned? Sorry I pissed in it last time.

You know I'm a good guy, don't ya?

Character reference:
Mate, father, brother, whatever.

*

Out of jail now, yeah.
Only thing they love in there is labels.
I ain't going back.

You believe in me, don't ya?
No messin' this time.
Not leaving the house unless I have to.
You won't see me unless it's a job interview.
You know I can sell more than anybody else, don't ya?
You know I can sell more than anybody else, don't ya?
You know I can sell more than anybody else, don't ya?

You know I can sell more than anybody else, don't ya?
You know
I can sell
more than
anybody else,
don't ya?

You still working with kids?
You still doing that?

Must be knackering.

I couldn't do that.

I dunno why you do it?

I run my own business now.
Mum's proud.
I bought my own suit.

Mad that, innit?

DREAMS

I dream:

I scream.

I come out strong on the mic -

like
Public Enemy, Hammersmith Apollo,
Aswad, Brixton Academy,
Kano's legendary 'Fire in the booth' on BBC Radio 1Xtra,
Jay Z at Glastonbury,
or him doing 'the Paris song' with an on-the-edge Kanye West.
How many rewinds did they get? 17.

I wake up.

I feel
like me on a really good day,
me on my best day,

me when my boss hired the Xmas brass band
just to celebrate my glory.
The best £30 he'd ever spent.

I dream:

I scream.

I come out strong on the mic -

like
Little Richard - any gig, any time, any place, anywhere.
Prince - any gig, any time, any place, anywhere.
Stevie Wonder - any gig, any time, any place, anywhere.

I wake up.

Today:
I feel like I've never had a good day.

Today:
I can't even get out of bed.

DELAY

Remember
how
we said
we'd be
so different

and

ended up
like everybody else?

We simply delayed the inevitable.

SCARF

I

Nobody really likes those half-and-half football scarves.
You know, the ones with 2 teams on them.

It's alright for a football fight that doesn't mean anything,
like Rochdale vs Grimsby
but when it's Man City Blue vs United Red,
nobody wants a half-and-half football scarf, not really.

Standing in court having to choose sides
never gets any easier at 7, 14 or 21.

Seeing the ones who you've loved
and loved you back in equal measure
bound by the feet, arms behind the back,
carried away twisting like a serpent
without knowing if they'll soon be wearing a black bag skin.

It never gets any easier at 7, 14, 21, 28

The glaring lights of the courtroom.
No one ever expects the child inquisition:

The crack of the ball against the post?
The crack of the skull against the wall?

Nobody likes the half-and-half football scarves.

Dad doesn't take me to play 5-a-side anymore.
Mum doesn't know what the off-side rule is.

II

30,000 screaming,
5000 silent in the 'away end'.

1 child screaming,
13 opposition - Judge and jury in the 'away end'.

Can I bring on a sub off the bench, m'lord?
Can I bring on a substitute from the bench?

Can I bring on a sub off the bench, your honour?
Can I bring on a substitute from the bench?

Winning is losing and losing is winning.

Can I have a new scarf, new mummy and daddy, your grace?
Can I bring on a sub off the bench?

III

Football is just chess with pieces that run.
We get to show
our aggression,
our vulnerability
without scaring anybody.
Yelling with 60,000 or yelling at the results
on TV in the front room.

This is our safe space.
Never deny a man his football.
Never ask him about his scarf.
Never ask him the score.

TV

TV don’t make no sense.

Deep plunging neckline,
titillate tantalise,
imagine the head in the trough to have a nibble? Yes.

Demure Muslim Headscarf allowed? No.

TV don’t make no sense.

Naked Attraction:

Game-show to select a sex-mate.
See all the bits before
you hear the words or see the face.

TV don’t make no sense

Oscar winners
getting paid millions
to play homeless people.

TV don’t make no sense.

Gogglebox:

Your reaction
to a facial expression
on another TV show
makes you a star?
TV don’t make no sense.

An actor gave the funeral eulogy
about the man he played
on the big screen.
Reincarnation 2.0

Life don’t make no sense.

TUNES

Labels?
Some people are more obsessed by the pressing,
the reissue and what the sleeve looks like
than the tunes.

I love music.
I love it, love it, love it.

I can't play a note or sing though
otherwise I'd have been an indie rock star for sure.

I couldn't find a girlfriend on my radio wavelength
in this funky town
so I went on the net,
found one who was into me
and all things indie.

I didn't tell anyone about it,
not until I was sure it was going to work.

Phone.
Text.
Email.
Video chat.
None of this replaces being with someone.

I jumped on a plane,
I took longer and longer holidays
from my graphics job designing record covers,
to see her and her kids.
I waved my old life goodbye.

I got a Green Card and stayed.
I was a loving husband and stepfather.

I suppose your looking for a sad ending
or some crazy twist?
There isn't one.

Me and her? It didn't work out,
but her children still phone, visit, call me daddy
and sing my favourite songs
on my birthday.

4.WORK+MONEY

#MONEY

The rules:

Why is it always about
how much money you make?

That's just the way it is.
It's the way it's always been
Don't ask me.
I don't make the rules.

BREAKIN' 01

5am.
Don't you mean 4.30?
I overslept.
It wasn't me.
I'm not denying anything.
It wasn't me.
All black to blend in with the night,
but it's already dawn, the first cars are on the road.
Is that a problem?
Doesn't matter.
It wasn't me.
I was safely tucked up in bed.
Snoring loudly.
Sinusitis, all my housemates know about it.
It's well documented.
I made sure of that.
By the way,
let me just remind you,
it wasn't me.
I wasn't there.
This is all hypothetical.
It's all conjecture.
I know some very important people
and more importantly,
some very important people know me.
So let me reiterate -
all this never happened.

The all-black clothing, the black bag,
the hammer, the cracked glass, the entry,
the jewellery, the sprayed-gold chain
overvalued for insurance purposes.

That was never, under any circumstances,
me.

Up the road from me,
which could be done and dusted, back in half an hour
maybe a close twenty-five if I sprinted.
Didn't I mention my long-term asthma condition?
It's well documented.
Ask my doctor.
I made sure of that.
Don't forget my sinusitis.
Me?
I yawned, saw my housemates for breakfast.
I always do my washing on a morning.
Jogging for fitness? Me? No, no way.
Keeping fit is for desperate people.
I never look desperate.

I
always look chilled.
Same look.
Same haircut.
Same clothes.
Let me repeat again.
And again.
And again.
It wasn't me.
I wasn't there.

But I could theoretically, hypothetically tell you
how
someone with my abilities
could plan and execute such a caper.
Theoretically, hypothetically
of course.
No more than that
because
I would never,
never ever,
ever ever ever,
break into someone's house,
even though I have no money
for food, drink, shoes, girlfriends, drugs.
I keep myself to myself.

Ask my friend, my buddy - he's a good character witness.

BREAKIN' 02

A letter:
A summons,
A Court date.
Wrong address, misspelt name,
it found its way to me anyway.
In court, for money owed - to you?
That wasn't your idea, was it?

That's fuckin' brazen.
If ever there was a signal
that too much drug-taking
can fuck up all a man's senses,
this has got to be it.

You
gave me money
to fake
a break-in
at your house.

You
didn't get as much
on the insurance
as you thought.

I
only got
Beer-money anyway.

Now
you come after me

to take my last pennies
cos you think
I've got a good job.

Is that how buddies do things now?

You roped in a friend who's a trainee lawyer.
He don't smoke it, like you still cane it.
He's just doing this for the practice,
for old times sake.

Is that really you, grinning?

So
you want me
to walk
into the court room
and
NOT
tell them
what really happened?

You
want me to hand over
all that I have.
No fuss, no fight,
no buddy love.

That wasn't your idea, was it?

At which
all-night all-day
24-hour

Hashish LSD
magic-mushroom soup session
did you concoct this scam?
Where was my invite?

It didn't work out
how you planned it
in your head, did it?

Lawyers (even trainees)
aren't cheap.
The truth hurts
your brain and your wallet, doesn't it?

You want to go for a pint with me?
For old time's sake?
No.
Not enough hours in this or any universe, buddy.

II

I walk away
me and the trainee lawyer in the same direction
talking about time-wasting,
talking about his wife, his kid,
how nobody canes it like they used to cane it
cos nobody can lock-down a job,
come up with a masterplan for life
and the lives of their kin
if they are blasting out brain cells
like there's no tomorrow.

We left you.

That's not how you planned it in your head, is it?

Do you even remember it right through your drug-fuelled haze?

now all that exists of you is this:
No name, no detail, no insurance policy number, no memory.

PAY THE COST TO BE THE BOSS

I never understood my magnificent brain
until the day my heart broke.

My body had a fight with itself,

argued about stress, brain wanted to chill –
the rest of me said to keep going.
Bits of me you can't see were the casualties.

My brain:
made it clear
It was the one running things.
The boss of the whole show.

Still I didn't listen to the signals.

I thought I could push it, instead of listening.

I went to the doctor, he gave me some tablets.
Sweet ones, tasty ones.
Then the things I took for granted:

the Lopsided grin, smile
the quick fire jokes
the ideas
the caring
the crying
the wanting to create
the capacity to engage - to want to live,

decayed piece by piece,
one tablet at a time.

The doctor said the meds were working
cos my face was looking fine.
One even symmetrical expression:
Comatose lama.

*

Give me back
my dilapidation,
broken bits
my ability to be me.

People will just have
to drive,
work harder,
dig deeper
to find
the interior beautiful me
and my magnificent brain

instead of stopping at the first juncture.

Give me
the greatness
the looseness
the fire
the highs
the lows

because they all make me who I am.

The only problems come when I don't listen to the needs
of my magnificent brain

or listen to people who want a symmetrical face,
file me under dysfunctional.

Scientists know
a symmetrical face is a natural impossibility.

Give me the nature of my head
with all the blues it entails.
Keep your pink noise, your white distortion.

RANT

I don't get tired
I breathe through my eyes.

Can a hairdresser give themselves a haircut?
They can cut the fringe but can't do the back.
You need to trim yours now. Get the hair out of your eyes.

You can't see how great you are
cos you're running in your own lane.
Look how far you've come?
Other people ain't got that.
Other people can't do that.
It's like on the starting line and you got to race to a 100.
You're passing people starting from zero.
You're passing people starting from one,
people who've had every advantage,
people who were running before the gun went off
and you were starting from 'minus 50'.
In real terms, you're passing Usain Bolt.

You are world class.
You're: A.
You're: A star.
You're: A star star.

You don't believe me or your mates about how good you are
cos we're your mates.
It's only when somebody who ain't us
tells you the same thing
that you believe
and when you see them a few times,

you don't believe them either.

Easy way -
write it down.
Take your name off, call yourself 'Mr A'
then mail it to somebody you don't know,
who knows about these things.
Say you're asking for a friend.
Write down all you've done,
how far you've come from your starting block.

We're talking: A
We're talking: A star,
We're talking: A star star.

You're lapping people,
lapping people for real.
So we don't do no pity party.
That's not our style.
So you gotta get out of bed, you hear me?

You're magnificent.

When you wake up the first thing you gotta tell yourself is,
'I am fantastic - no ifs no buts.'
If people don't like it they can fuck off.

I can't hear you. You need to say,

'I am fantastic - no ifs no buts.'
'I am fantastic - no ifs no buts.'
'I am fantastic - no ifs no buts.'
'I am fantastic - no ifs no buts.'

If people don't like it, they can fuck off.

You think I talk too much?
I must be knackered?
This isn't work.
How can telling the truth be work?

5.RACE

#BLACK BROWN RED YELLOW WHITE

The rules:

Why is it always about

Race?

That's just the way it is.
It's the ways it's always been.
Don't ask me.
I don't make the rules.

HOW MAN WAS MADE (TEESSIDE REMIX)

We made you on red fire whisky
and Newcastle Brown ale.

We made you with overproof rum
and golden parmos.

We made you with the cool afro jazz of the desert shabeens
and the ruckus of Irish pubs.

We made you with snow-covered Ayresome Park nights,
yelling at referees from the terraces
and the sweet samba of Juninho's goals.

We made you,

your mother and me
with our own sugar cane dance, our own makossa.

We made you with love.
Whatever others may call you,

the name we gave you
means 'the best of both worlds'
in the language of the heart.

CLUB

Remember
the time
they wouldn't
let you
into the club

but
the DJ
was playing
your tunes?

BLACK MAN INDEX BMI

Check the internet.
Check the stats.
Check the B.M.I
Black Man Index a.k.a How British am I feeling today?

Sir Trevor McDonald reading the news?
45%.
Stephen Lawrence death?
10%.
Stephen Lawrence murderers jailed?
60%.

Sir Lenny Henry
followed by Ainsley Harriott on prime time TV?
80%.
Ainsley Harriott
mistaken for Lenny Henry on the news?
-5%.

Enoch Powell 'Rivers of Blood' speech
locked away in the Black Cultural Archives?
90%.

Enoch Powell's speech
reanimated on the BBC in 2018?
-666%.

500 Black man deaths in police custody,
no charges, no explanation?
-7777 %.

Windrush children denied healthcare?
Windrush children denied pensions?
Windrush Children being deported?

I can't check it.
I broke the computer.
It makes me

ANGRY

like I wanna do something with an AK47 machine gun,
instead of yelling down an SM58 microphone.

OK.
Breathe deep.
De-stress.

Forget local.
Go international.

Travon Martin unarmed,
gunned down by a cop for no good reason.
Obama heckled in the senate?
Eric Garner's last words:

'I can't breathe.'

Windrush Children Deportees Resettlement Booklet and DVD
Mandatory study UK Government guide:
'Try to be Jamaican,' it says.
'Use local accents and dialects
(overseas accents can attract unwanted attention).'

I’ve got to give up the internet.
I’ve got to go off-grid for my own piece of mind.
I’ve got to give up checking
my B.M.I.

6.SEX+RELATIONSHIPS

#SEX

The rules:

Why is it always about

Sex?

That's just the way it is.
It's the ways it's always been.
Don't ask me.
I don't make the rules.

TO WHOM IT MAY CONCERN

I wanted to write about you
but I am a different man.

I wanted to write about you.
I really did.
I'm sitting here with a pen in my hand ready to let it all out,
dance around the clichés,
say how you were the best, how it felt to be with you,
but there is nothing.

If people ask about us
I refer to you by your full name.
Not first name, pet name or lovers name.
Maybe there is a scientific name for this?

When I mention your name in my head
I wait for the tingle in my hands again,
the hairs on my arms to stand up,
a ripple of sweat to roll off my neck.
Nothing.
There must be a scientific name for this?

Your old photograph captures our best days
Black and white so I don't know what colour the sun was.

So what was the point of that?
Marking time?
Is this what happens to all great romances?
All major dalliances?

I am a different man.

It takes seven years to replace all the atoms in one body.
There must be a scientific name for this?

I am a different man:
different molecules,
same frame,
tweaked design.

So I must presume
after all these years, days, minutes, seconds,
the science
has named this

the end.

CONFESSIONS OF A SAINT

Words brought us together, words ripped us apart.
Words brought us together, words tore us apart.

I stretched to the top of the tower racks on a summer day.
Blew the dust from long forgotten first-editions.

People look for answers in the height of mountains,
the tallest bookshelves
yet pass over the mystery of themselves without a thought.

Our eyes met over the books of *St. Augustine*,
Transactional analysis - the psychology of talking,
Body language - the psychology of physical action.

How to pray, how to believe, how to listen,
how to read bodies.

Papers, research, any excuse to delve deeper -

I think she knew that?
I'm sure she knew that?

On the first late session -
The corridor of lights turned off.
Closer

Click
Step
Click
Step

Only one overhead illumination

My pen
My scrawl on paper
The words of St. Augustine make no sense

> *"I was not yet in love, yet I loved to love…*
> *I sought what I might love, in love with loving."*

Her hair smelt of ripe bananas.
Her body smelt of palm wine.
Her kisses tasted of

the words that brought us together
and the senses that tore us apart.

We studied the tones of speech,
higher, lower and the layers of subtext in-between.

We studied bodies
how we read them
between the bookshelves
and the night-time alcoves.

Last one out turn off the lights above.
click step click step.

The words brought us together,
words tore us apart.

The words of St. Augustine made no sense:

"I was not yet in love, yet I loved to love...
I sought what I might love, in love with loving."

How do we pray?
How do we venerate?
Are all loves created equal?

"The measure of love is
to love without measure."

I couldn't answer.

I never finished my notes
In the dark.

She was gone.

All that is left (on a winter's day) is
the relic of an expired library card.

FANCY THAT?

Remember that time with the lads?
You got the beers in.
We all joked we thought you were gay
cos we never saw you chatting up a woman
then you pulled the most beautiful girl in the world.

So hot
she make a darkie forget about skin tone.
So hot
she make a batty-man straight.
So hot
she make a thug-rapper write sonnets.
So hot
she make a happy man want to check her out,
even though he's already loved up
long-time no-problem no-wandering eye.

We were all jealous.
Of course this is real life so there were obstacles.
She had a kid but that didn't faze you.

We asked were you 'getting some' and you said

'YEAH'

despite all the complications.
Catholic upbringing had messed her up,
she'd got pregnant the first time she'd had sex,
but hey,
step back,
she was still

the most beautiful girl in the world.

So hot
she make a darkie forget about skin tone.
So hot
she make a batty-man straight.
So hot
she make a thug-rapper write sonnets.
So hot
she make a happy man want to check her out,
even though he's already loved up
long-time no-problem no-wandering eye.

The most beautiful girl in the world?

We are talking
breath-holding
head-turning
stunning with or without make up.
You had the whole crew jealous
but you just played it cool

like a man.

Remember our friend? He was seeing her sister who,
to be fair was alright, but not in the same league.
She said you and the hot girl –
in the same bed all week but nothing's happening.

We grilled you
and you said,
'Hey, she's had problems.
It's not all about

the quick shag, the wam-bam thank you ma'am'

cos after all she is
the most beautiful girl in the world.

Those were the days.

Do you remember that time
when you got the pints in and told us she was perfect?

So perfect cos people stopped asking questions
cos you actually liked men,
shagged them on the down-low in the gay clubs in the week,
hung out with us on the weekend.

Remember that time
you introduced us to your husband?
Nice bloke.
Do you remember that time you got the beers in?

SEX 101

Remember
when you said

she could do
what she liked

as long
as she
always came back?

She never came back.

SCRATCHED

He never recovered, not really, not fully.
I could hear it his voice I could see it in his moist eyes,
I could hear it in the music he played.

He'd put a lifetime of work - his 12inch vinyl collection,
in a warehouse
and given the key to charity.

Maybe every tune reminded him of her,
or her and the kids
or just the kids.

They'd had their problems but doesn't every couple,
every family?

But he'd put all his records in a lock-up
and given away the key.

When did he crack? When did his vinyl get scratched?

Was it when her tribe of brothers beat him up?

Was it when he'd got back home,
discovered his high-spending argumentative wife
had moved out and sold the house?

Was it when he found himself on a friend's couch
with no phone credit to call his kids on Christmas Day
but they never called anyway?

Was it when he discovered digital
didn’t sound as good as analogue?
MP3 don't sound as good as wax?

Is it when they got divorced?

Is it when she moved the kids to a different town
and he couldn’t afford the trainfare?

Is it when she said she was going to change his children’s surname,
erase every trace of his lineage, genetic existence?

It takes seven years to change every molecule in the body.

How many years?
He still looks fucked, looks dejected,
he deejays with digital only.

He’s got a fiancé now, she's nice I hear.
African - same country, different tribe.

He’s building a house made of moulded vinyl plastic bricks,
the grooves slide together when you blow the dust off.

He's waiting to be a different man.
I can hear it in his voice, I can see it in his eyes,
I can here it in the 8bit music he plays.

Teddy Pendergrass porch,
Artful Dodger Garage door,
A path made of Mariah Carey
leading to a house made of moulded vinyl plastic bricks.

Spare room in the back, ready for his kids to visit.
They must be about 30-years-old now.

LEAP

Remember how she proposed after 20 years of bliss
cos it was a leap year.

Remember how you were divorced
365 days later.

THE PUSH AND PULL OF THE AMEN BREAK

We argue all the time,
blazing rows in the street, don't care who's looking.
The glass bottle of perfume
costing more of my salary than I want to remember
gives the run-down street
the fragrance of sun-drenched beach holidays.

We walk in opposite directions.
You go to your mother's for the weekend.
I got the house to myself.
No 'Mama Mia' soundtrack tonight.
No 'Dancing Queen', 'Saturday Night Fever' tonight.
Only the tunes I got mad love for, getting played tonight,
Liquid Drum and bass tunes as loud as I like.

Neighbours pumping their fists on the door
in time with the beats,
but I need a sound system vibe
to be as happy as I like.

I go out:

She
is not like you.
She
smiles.
She laughs at my jokes,
even when the club music batters our ears.
We exchange numbers.
She calls me or I call her,
I can't remember.

She
Is not like you
We arrange to meet.
What does that mean?
I put on aftershave.
What does that mean?
I check my profile in the mirror.
I look good (stomach pulled in or relaxed,
before or after a whisky chaser).
What does that mean?
I check my wallet for a pack of 3.
What does that mean?
I take money out of the bank - untraceable.
I iron my shirt.
What does that mean?
She
is not you.
We
sit in the pub.
I buy the drinks - cash, untraceable.
She smiles.
She flicks her hair,
I know what this means.
The jukebox - quiet enough for every sentence to be heard,
over the 'Amen 178bpm Breakbeat'.
I know what this means.

She
is not you.
And?
I could have -
but I didn't
because

she
Isn't -
wasn't
You.
I know what that means.

It means Goldie's 'Inner City Life'
playing when we walk down the aisle.
It means a wedding cake shaped like turntables.
It means a Rave MC doing the best man's speech
wearing 1970s sparkly-white suit with flared trousers,
a Junglist Soundsystem playing Abba at the reception.

There is a quiet corner of our high street
with boarded up windows
and cold rain
that will always smell of our sun-drenched kisses.

YEARS

After all these years
I still fancy you,
want to make love with you,
want to have sex with you,
fuck with you.
That's not normal, is it?

RUSSIAN DOLL

I don't have a type.

You are my last girlfriend's brain in my first girlfriend's body,
overlaid with your own problems.

It's alright,

I'll see myself out.

SHOPPING

Remember,
I love you

so much

I go shopping
with you
on my day off.

TOXIC SECRETS

A secret shared is a problem halved.
Who told you that?

There's no easy way to talk about rape, is there?
You can't sugar-coat it, drop some funny one-liners,
casually change the subject over pints or dinner or TV?

You asked me if I was a strong man?
I thought you were talking about my muscles.
We were already beneath the sheets.
Am I a man you could trust?
I thought you were talking about my honesty.
We were already beneath the sheets.

'You could tell me anything,' I said.
You said:
Who, how, where, when.
We were already beneath the sheets.

You said you
loved me
trusted me
to keep the secrets.

We would always be the same, we would never change.

I wondered how many other lovers you'd told
before or after
underneath the sheets

and if they all thought the same as me.

Am I strong enough?
How do I act, what do I say?

Double-back, re-check all comedies.
Both your hands on the remote control
instead of on me.
Are the teardrops from the trauma
or the romantic film
we watch
above the sheets?

A secret shared is a problem halved.
Who told you that?

MAN UP

I

Don't hate the player, hate the game.
I make up the rules.

I never got my fair share,
didn't have the body for it,
the gift of the gab or the swagger for it,
not like some other chat-pon-de-mic MCs.
Me?
3 girlfriends at the same time.
No? Yes. Really? Yes.
Why?
Cos I argued and won
cos I argued and lost
cos I was bored
cos she was bleeding
cos I needed to test my persona
cos it's about levels
cos it's about bragging rights
that need some foundation to be built upon
cos I'm a man with simple tastes, a lover of easy victories.

Oh I nearly forgot,
that wasn't me.

II

I met her at a party, got a number, the rest is history.
I met her at a party, friend of a friend, the rest is history.

I met her when I woke up, I'd drank too much,
she was in my bed, the rest is history.

Those antics fade to the back of sober memory
dispersed amongst the stars.

III

I trudge along
up the steps of the weather-beaten shack,
faded peeling wallpaper inside,
empty home-brew bottles outside.

Father - Bones rattling around in a mottled-skin bag
held together by the pressure of anger,
dementia carving tunnels through his brain,
remembering fights from another era.

Is this what old swagger looks like?
Is this what winning looks like?

He has a new woman bleeding him dry,
spending my dead mother's money.

'I met her when I woke up, I'd drunk too much.
She was in my house and in my bank account, the rest is history'.

Is he the man I am destined to be?

She: his latest '*now and forever'* makes small talk,
tiny vampire words I'm not interested in.

Puncture wounds
where the anti-viral HIV drugs go in
or the blood comes out?

A nurse paid to watch the decay,
mop up the puss,
pretend to love more than the debits.

She'll be gone as soon as he runs into debt.

Father - Bones rattling around in a crusty-skin bag
held together by the pressure of anger
over not getting his dues.
But maybe he did.

IV

I met her.
Her story - *I never called back.*
I met her,
Her story - *I never called back.*

'He was quiet, funny, aloof, angry, distant,'

Except…
Her,
her story,

'He called back,
said he'd had stuff to sort out.
Man stuff. New rules to write.'

V

I parade her in front of people I don't know.
I turn down the secluded romantic candle-lit dinner she offers.

I want her
to be seen with me.

That is my only protection
because I fear slipping, forgetting,
failing to remember

after an argument I've won,
after an argument I've lost.

Sliding,
failing to remember,
winning at the undercover swagger persona
only leads to losing.

I'm not crazy enough to think I can rewrite those rules.

SALES

My kids:
I want them to be
strong, clever, independently minded, happy
and stylish dressers.

Do I want a say in who they marry?
Of course I do.
They take a long time to make -
longer to manufacture than a Rolls-Royce
and three times as precious.

Would you give your car and your house
away to any flash salesman?
Read the terms and conditions?

bamboozled by the spin.

I want a say in who they marry:
it takes years to get wisdom,
you can lose it in one night in a reckless storm
with too many mojitos then a 24hour chapel in Vegas.

Did I let my parents have a say in my relationships?
Hell, no.
Have you seen how they dress?
I wouldn't even let them choose my shoes or my GCSEs.

SHEPHERDESS

Under a brilliant red sky,
nobody can tell the time
except an experienced shepherd
or shepherdess

Clouds, flock and lambs
look the same from the hillside
the shape, the form under the silver-white sheets
are known to only you and I

Reflections of our souls are in the movements
Reflections of our souls are in the whispers
Reflections of our souls are at the bottom of the bottle

Nobody can love me like you do

We can do everything
anything
except call this what it is

Tell ourselves bleached-white lies
Tell ourselves it doesn't really matter
Tell ourselves there are no strings

When you pull me under the covers again
we explore what it means

Just to be

You can guide me anywhere you want this to go
corralled into the cavern

penned in our room within a room

The shapes we form until dawn
What do you release in me?
What do I release in you?

Tell ourselves there are no strings

Tell ourselves we will never become undone
because we never promised to be bound

Never promised gold bands, beer-can ring pulls,
plastic screw-top lids

We always finish what we start

We only want the knowledge of time

Other animals, gin-soaked night-crawlers
know all the colours the sky makes
That's not us
Never meant to be us

Only ever knowing what a shepherdess knows:
leading
stroking
humming the commands
opening and closing the gate
when the sky is red.

So we can whistle long black lies at anytime the clock ticks
At anytime we desire
At anytime we want to escape

To our own fields

Nobody can love me like you
Nobody has loved me like you
Nobody

But it wasn't love

It was food, it was soul nutrition, it was desire

When it's finally over
We won't talk of this

We will be fragments of another life
We will be a shared anecdote
We will be a raised eyebrow at a memory
We will be a laugh under a solitary red sky for no damn reason
We will be 10pm till 6 in the morning
We will be crumpled sheets, an empty bottle of vodka
We will be gone

Nobody can love me like you do
Nobody has loved me like you
Nobody

But it wasn't love

It was food, it was soul, it was desire
It was sweat, it was hot skin
It was the cool breeze under guidance

It was - what we knew it was
temporary, necessary, beautiful

I'll say it again

it was
what we knew it was meant to be
built to be

Temporary, necessary, beautiful

gone

like

the drifting clouds
in a perfect ruby red sky.

SQUIGGLES

Labels are like posters,
you can draw all over them, squiggle all over them,
spray all over them any time you like.

You work with kids, yeah?
You work with kids like me, don't ya?

Don't worry about me
I like doodling, smoking spliffs
I'm always sorted,
got meself a nice girl, me princess.
She's still at school
I left early,
couldn't hack it, not interested.
Don't need it.
No jobs anyway.
I'm sorted.

Got tunes, got skateboard,
got roll-your-own, got grow-your-own.
Got me princess.

I'm gonna marry that girl, you'll see.
You don't believe me, do ya?
I'm gonna make an honest woman of her.

*

She's left me.
She says she ain't got another fella.
I don't believe her.

I heard her new bloke's called Billy Shakespeare.

I got to be honest.
I don't feel sorted,
even with the beers, the pills,
the roll-your-own, grow-your-own.
Even with the latest bangin' tune.

People notice my squiggles are shit now.
Got to knuckle down now.
Don't care about her now.

Got a new girl now.
She's proper fit,
I mean proper fit.
She knows how to roll em, ya get me?

Thing is, when I draw her, try to make a portrait of her,
it comes out looking like my old girl.

That ain't right, is it?

You work with people like me, don't ya?

I've blotted her out.
Extra-strength skunk.
Don't care if I don't hold it together,
all I ever wanted was my princess.

Saw myself in the mirror -
no amount of spray cans,
tattoos can cover up
how shit I'm looking.

One more blowback, for old times sake.
One more hot-knife, for old times sake.
One more night out with the lads, for old times sake.

Woke up with my head through a mirror.
10 hours in A&E,
can't remember what happened.

The lads said it was wild,
said my graffiti tag was mad large
(on the post office wall).

*

I'm keeping my stitched-up-head down now.
I'm Billy No-mates now.
Just me and doodles on pieces of paper now.

Going to college part-time now.
Going to university part-time now.
Trying hard, low-profile time now.
Going places where they call my sketch book, a portfolio now.

I saw her, my old princess
carrying a big bag of books.
She asked me if I was any good at portraits?
I said yeah.
She asked me
if I could design a tattoo
of her first love,
Old Billy.

I'll cut the story-squiggles short,
it's all about the vectors now,
Straight ahead,
I've got my own posters, a clothing label
and my princess back.

My biggest selling t-shirt is 'Romeo and Juliet'
as cool-kid skateboarders.
Mad that, innit?

ALLERGIES

Men don't skip. Why am I skipping?
That don't make no sense.

Food tastes better when you cook it.
You can't cook, everybody knows that. Ask the kids?
How many times have you burnt dinner?

My taste buds must be messed up.
They don't make no sense.

I'm watching the same shit Saturday night programs you do.
That don't make no sense.

I'm bothered by the fact I'm not bothered
by your stretch marks.
That don't make no sense.

That thing you do with flowers -
stick them in a water bottle
to sniff when your stuck at traffic lights.

That's sweet, even though it don't make no sense.

Anyway.
You know how you're always telling me to look after myself?
I've been to the doctor.
He says it's probably allergies.

He's given me a big prescription.
I've got an Epi-pen (for emergencies) and anti-histamines.

ROLL

Remember when you had a dream:
she was married
with loads of kids
to some dickhead
in another town
then you woke up sweating
like you'd had a real fuckin' nightmare.

Then you rolled over in bed:
she was there,
snoring her head off.

She wasn't married.
She didn't have kids.
A mental dream, wasn't it?

If I were you, I'd see someone about that.

7.DEATH

#DEATH

You can skip this part if you want to.
Section it, compartmentalise it if you want to.

None of us are getting out of here alive.
Each and every one of us is going to spend
our last days having our bottoms wiped
by an immigrant on minimum wage.

There is no bonus for wiping the dribble off our chins.
or listening to our dementia-afflicted stories.

NO QUEUE JUMPING

What did you go and do that for?
A permanent solution to a temporary problem.

I have very few rules:
be kind to others and no queue jumping.

I don't want to see you before your mother,
father, gran and grandpa.

I don't want see you knocking on the door
begging to come in.

I said, I'll see you when I want to see you.

There's a reason why
the Pope
used to be
a night-club bouncer.

What did you go and do that for?

You're gonna have people
wondering
if there was something
they could have done,
anything
they could've done
different.

You're giving me work to do now.
Reincarnation ain't easy.

I'm gonna have to slice up
the memory of you,

distribute it to all the people who
loved you, cared for you, prayed for you.

And when I send you back in some obscure form
your family and friends recognise
in the face of your unborn cousins,

Remember these words:
feel free to shout them out loud
anytime you feel bad -
no queue jumping.

GUITAR HERO

Remember, Strat Boy?
Legend.
So rich he got the first beers in, no problem.
Legend.
Split up from his live-in long-term girlfriend –
remained friends.
Straight amicable.
Legend.
She got fed up of him playing guitar in bed:
Strats, Telecasters, Fender Acoustics.
Legend.
Remember when he looked like an indie rockstar?
The only thing he loved more than maths and computers
was music and fishing.
He said he was gonna retire in a year, buy a boat,
sail around the coast of Ireland.
Has enough money for the rest of his life
and still get the beers in.
Legend.

Remember the stag do?
Fishing.
Scratch on his leg, we said
You ought to get that seen to.
All in good time.
All in due time.

Remember how, he remembered I didn't drink anymore,
when he got the beers in?
Legend.
Getting married wouldn't change anything.

We'd still meet up.
Anything to get out of shopping.
Legend.
Remember when you called on a summer day?
Strat Boy's in a coma
Looking like an out-of-condition rockstar.
Remember how he forgot about the maths,
the science of sepsis?
Remember who had to make the decision
to turn off the life-support machine?
Remember how you knew he was already gone.

Remember, Strat Boy.
Legend.

PEOPLE

Losing people
we love,

never gets
any easier

the older we get.

ENOUGH

Remember when I said, ‘I am enough’.
You said,
‘Have you been smoking some extra-strength weed?’
‘Are you banging a hippie chick?’

When we are sombre and sometimes sober
over the passing of our friends,
we hug and say, ‘enough is enough is enough’.

PUNCTUAL

I

You were on 'the one'
You bent the silver thick bass strings
like you could shape water with your thoughts.

You were on time - 6pm.
Always punctual.

The only bass player they'd ever had, who was.

'What did you do with the rest of your time?' they asked.

Back to the groove, the slap,
the zing, the pop, the funk,
the fretboard. The marked dark red wood
was a snake and you charmed it.

What did you do with the rest of your time?
9 to 5 like the rest?
Music your life?
Or just a hobby?
Or something more?

The crowd of 5:
the band's flatmates, hangers on

were dazzled and shared a pint –
the cut of the door takings, the winnings.

What happened to the band?

II

You saw her - by the bus stop,
by accident or design.

'Its late. The timetable's never accurate.'
'What do you expect for London?'

7 buses snarled up on some junction,
Some unspoken calamity.

She:
the old lead singer,
she'd been to your flat once.
'Pink walls,' she said,
'like a French tart's palace,' she laughed.

What do you expect for London?
What do you expect to get for these prices?

Whatever happened to that band,
when you were all on 'the one'?

Job?
9 to 5?
Hobbies?

Things
take up more than life?

'Doing much later?' she asked.
That's how you remembered it.

'We can see a band.'

Bus stop -
chances of delayed punctuality.

The band were tight.
'I'd give them lessons,' you said
to teach them how to find 'the one'.
They still had the dream though
and a crowd of smiles
paying more than beer money.

They were late for the encore.
Maybe it's the drugs?
Maybe it's London?

They were late for the encore.

Late,
so you walked her home,
'Because London can be dangerous
for people you don't know,' you said.

'Just a cup of coffee,' you said.
You commented on her wall paper.
Did she prefer pink?

'Remember when we bounced, grooved and laughed?'
"With the rest of the band,' she added.

Yes of course,
and when she nipped out
to the toilet

or top up her coffee,

you slipped under the covers

and she screamed.

Did she?
Did she?
Did she?

'But it's not like that',
you just wanted to feel comfy.
You talked from midnight til 9.

About -
how you haven't been feeling yourself lately.

How -

Time is taking up too much time,
the hours are slipping and the groove of life is wrong
and you didn't like pink, mauve or anything with a tint of red.

You hadn't been feeling yourself for a while.

Maybe take the anti-depressants again?
Maybe tell people about the anti-psychotic medication again?

But it takes away from
the zip, the zag, the ping,
the swoosh and the slickness of the groove.

Did her flatmates give you a lift home?

Can't remember?

Probably.

Buses aren't punctual these days.
Always some problem at a junction, snarling things up.

Always better to take the train,

they're always punctual -
almost as tight to the schedule as the Tokyo bullet train.
Now that's a city you'd like to see.
Maybe in your dreams?
Maybe if you win the lottery?

No matter what people say about London

and the profusion of red buses,
the trains are always on time –ish.

Tight to the track.

Punctual enough to know when you step out
it will be quick
it will be easy
it will be punctual.

The two sides of your brain keep arguing,
pulling you away from the groove will stop,
the daily disruption of peoples lives will go on.

III

Some people say they saw you checking your watch
before you jumped.

Some people say they saw you
with your eyes closed,

playing an imaginary bass guitar
for the final lock into the groove.

For ‘the one’.

You thought you were in heaven
when you heard the sound
of the thin reedy voice.
You thought God would have more bass.

‘We regret to inform you,’ it said,
‘due to Industrial Action there will be no trains.
Sorry for any inconvenience.’

8.END

ROCKET-MAN (ONE LIGHT, ONE MIC AND A STORY)

Remember we've got a plan for when we die, mate
cos the life we've lived it's been crazy, dysfunctional,
it's been magnificent
and we want to go out with a bang.

Mental health?
Yeah, somebody's got to sort it so it might as well be you.

But I digress
The plan:

after all the bits of me that are still useful have been taken out,
put the rest in a rocket -
The biggest firework you can find and shoot it up.

You've got to go out with a bang, yeah
not a whimper.

Then afterwards:
free bar,
juice if you want it.

Good tunes, one spotlight and a mic.

People will get up and tell stories.

Somebody's bound to say something
nobody's heard before.

It'll be fun.

It'll be entertaining.
There'll be tunes.
Shame I won't be there.

Will people tell the truth on the mic?
Does it really matter?

Never let the truth get in the way of a good story.

A BIGGER BANG

I

How did this universe end and another one start?
Not with a bang but a whisper.

Phonecall:
when are you coming up?
I recognised
your song,
your graffiti,
your tag, your label
your squiggles on the side of post offices
and in the valentine cards.
I recognised you beneath the layers –
your dance, your makossa.

We can lie and do nothing.
Is this a love thing?

No, I said.
Never trust the scribblings of a drunk broke man.

II

How did this universe end and another one start?
with pints, whisky chasers and juice
lined up on the bar for friends,
whilst me and her went on a shopping trip.

How did this universe end and another one start?
With a dream, unplugging the mic and turning off the spotlight.

JOKE OUTRO

This,
like many things in a messy life,
started with a joke
and got out of control.

I found a way of
pulling all the strings together
and tying up the loose ends.

A BIGGER QUESTION

How will your new universe start?

www.ingramcontent.com/pod-product-compliance
Ingram Content Group UK Ltd.
Pitfield, Milton Keynes, MK11 3LW, UK
UKHW020128250726
13967UKWH00002B/530